My Anxiety Journal

This Belongs To:

_____

DATE: __/__/__   SUN   MON   TUE   WED   THU   FRI   SAT

Anxiety
Notes

ACTIVITY LEVEL

MOOD

ENERGY

SLEEP

SYMPTOMS

TRIGGERS

COPING SKILLS

MINDFULNESS EXERCISES

DATE: __/__/__   SUN   MON   TUE   WED   THU   FRI   SAT

Anxiety Notes

ACTIVITY LEVEL

MOOD

ENERGY

SLEEP

TRIGGERS

SYMPTOMS

COPING SKILLS

MINDFULNESS EXERCISES

DATE: __/__/__   SUN   MON   TUE   WED   THU   FRI   SAT

Anxiety Notes

ACTIVITY LEVEL

MOOD

ENERGY

SLEEP

SYMPTOMS

TRIGGERS

COPING SKILLS

MINDFULNESS EXERCISES

DATE: __/__/__   SUN   MON   TUE   WED   THU   FRI   SAT

Anxiety
Notes

ACTIVITY LEVEL

MOOD

ENERGY

SLEEP

TRIGGERS

SYMPTOMS

COPING SKILLS

MINDFULNESS EXERCISES

DATE: __/__/__   SUN   MON   TUE   WED   THU   FRI   SAT

Anxiety Notes

ACTIVITY LEVEL

MOOD

ENERGY

SLEEP

SYMPTOMS

TRIGGERS

COPING SKILLS

MINDFULNESS EXERCISES

DATE: __/__/__   SUN   MON   TUE   WED   THU   FRI   SAT

Anxiety
Notes

ACTIVITY LEVEL

MOOD

ENERGY

SLEEP

TRIGGERS

SYMPTOMS

COPING SKILLS

MINDFULNESS EXERCISES

DATE: __/__/__   SUN   MON   TUE   WED   THU   FRI   SAT

Anxiety
Notes

ACTIVITY LEVEL

MOOD

ENERGY

SLEEP

SYMPTOMS

TRIGGERS

COPING SKILLS

MINDFULNESS EXERCISES

DATE: __/__/__   SUN   MON   TUE   WED   THU   FRI   SAT

Anxiety Notes

ACTIVITY LEVEL

MOOD

ENERGY

SLEEP

TRIGGERS

SYMPTOMS

COPING SKILLS

MINDFULNESS EXERCISES

DATE: __/__/__   SUN   MON   TUE   WED   THU   FRI   SAT

Anxiety
Notes

ACTIVITY LEVEL

MOOD

ENERGY

SLEEP

SYMPTOMS

TRIGGERS

COPING SKILLS

MINDFULNESS EXERCISES

DATE: __/__/__   SUN   MON   TUE   WED   THU   FRI   SAT

Anxiety
Notes

ACTIVITY LEVEL

MOOD

ENERGY

SLEEP

TRIGGERS

SYMPTOMS

COPING SKILLS

MINDFULNESS EXERCISES

DATE: __/__/__   SUN   MON   TUE   WED   THU   FRI   SAT

Anxiety
Notes

ACTIVITY LEVEL

MOOD

ENERGY

SLEEP

SYMPTOMS

TRIGGERS

COPING SKILLS

MINDFULNESS EXERCISES

DATE: __/__/__   SUN   MON   TUE   WED   THU   FRI   SAT

Anxiety
Notes

ACTIVITY LEVEL

MOOD

ENERGY

SLEEP

TRIGGERS

SYMPTOMS

COPING SKILLS

MINDFULNESS EXERCISES

DATE: __/__/__   SUN   MON   TUE   WED   THU   FRI   SAT

Anxiety
Notes

ACTIVITY LEVEL

MOOD

ENERGY

SLEEP

SYMPTOMS

TRIGGERS

COPING SKILLS

MINDFULNESS EXERCISES

DATE: __/__/__   SUN   MON   TUE   WED   THU   FRI   SAT

Anxiety
Notes

ACTIVITY LEVEL

MOOD

ENERGY

SLEEP

TRIGGERS

SYMPTOMS

COPING SKILLS

MINDFULNESS EXERCISES

DATE: __/__/__   SUN   MON   TUE   WED   THU   FRI   SAT

Anxiety
Notes

ACTIVITY LEVEL

MOOD

ENERGY

SLEEP

SYMPTOMS

TRIGGERS

COPING SKILLS

MINDFULNESS EXERCISES

DATE: __/__/__   SUN   MON   TUE   WED   THU   FRI   SAT

Anxiety
Notes

ACTIVITY LEVEL

MOOD

ENERGY

SLEEP

TRIGGERS

SYMPTOMS

COPING SKILLS

MINDFULNESS EXERCISES

DATE: __/__/__   SUN   MON   TUE   WED   THU   FRI   SAT

Anxiety Notes

ACTIVITY LEVEL

MOOD

ENERGY

SLEEP

SYMPTOMS

TRIGGERS

COPING SKILLS

MINDFULNESS EXERCISES

DATE: __/__/__   SUN   MON   TUE   WED   THU   FRI   SAT

Anxiety
Notes

ACTIVITY LEVEL

MOOD

ENERGY

SLEEP

TRIGGERS

SYMPTOMS

COPING SKILLS

MINDFULNESS EXERCISES

DATE: __/__/__   SUN   MON   TUE   WED   THU   FRI   SAT

Anxiety
Notes

ACTIVITY LEVEL

MOOD

ENERGY

SLEEP

SYMPTOMS

TRIGGERS

COPING SKILLS

MINDFULNESS EXERCISES

DATE: __/__/__   SUN   MON   TUE   WED   THU   FRI   SAT

Anxiety
Notes

ACTIVITY LEVEL

MOOD

ENERGY

SLEEP

TRIGGERS

SYMPTOMS

COPING SKILLS

MINDFULNESS EXERCISES

DATE: __/__/__   SUN   MON   TUE   WED   THU   FRI   SAT

Anxiety
Notes

ACTIVITY LEVEL

MOOD

ENERGY

SLEEP

SYMPTOMS

TRIGGERS

COPING SKILLS

MINDFULNESS EXERCISES

DATE: __/__/__   SUN   MON   TUE   WED   THU   FRI   SAT

Anxiety Notes

ACTIVITY LEVEL

MOOD

ENERGY

SLEEP

TRIGGERS

SYMPTOMS

COPING SKILLS

MINDFULNESS EXERCISES

DATE: __/__/__   SUN   MON   TUE   WED   THU   FRI   SAT

Anxiety Notes

ACTIVITY LEVEL

MOOD

ENERGY

SLEEP

SYMPTOMS

TRIGGERS

COPING SKILLS

MINDFULNESS EXERCISES

DATE: __/__/__   SUN   MON   TUE   WED   THU   FRI   SAT

Anxiety
Notes

ACTIVITY LEVEL

MOOD

ENERGY

SLEEP

TRIGGERS

SYMPTOMS

COPING SKILLS

MINDFULNESS EXERCISES

DATE: __/__/__   SUN   MON   TUE   WED   THU   FRI   SAT

Anxiety
Notes

ACTIVITY LEVEL

MOOD

ENERGY

SLEEP

SYMPTOMS

TRIGGERS

COPING SKILLS

MINDFULNESS EXERCISES

DATE: __/__/__   SUN   MON   TUE   WED   THU   FRI   SAT

Anxiety Notes

ACTIVITY LEVEL

MOOD

ENERGY

SLEEP

TRIGGERS

SYMPTOMS

COPING SKILLS

MINDFULNESS EXERCISES

DATE: __/__/__   SUN   MON   TUE   WED   THU   FRI   SAT

Anxiety
Notes

ACTIVITY LEVEL

MOOD

ENERGY

SLEEP

SYMPTOMS

TRIGGERS

COPING SKILLS

MINDFULNESS EXERCISES

DATE: __/__/__   SUN   MON   TUE   WED   THU   FRI   SAT

Anxiety
Notes

ACTIVITY LEVEL

MOOD

ENERGY

SLEEP

TRIGGERS

SYMPTOMS

COPING SKILLS

MINDFULNESS EXERCISES

DATE: __/__/__   SUN   MON   TUE   WED   THU   FRI   SAT

Anxiety
Notes

ACTIVITY LEVEL

MOOD

ENERGY

SLEEP

SYMPTOMS

TRIGGERS

COPING SKILLS

MINDFULNESS EXERCISES

DATE: __/__/__   SUN   MON   TUE   WED   THU   FRI   SAT

Anxiety
Notes

— ACTIVITY LEVEL —

— MOOD —

— ENERGY —

— SLEEP —

— TRIGGERS —

— SYMPTOMS —

— COPING SKILLS —

— MINDFULNESS EXERCISES —

DATE: __/__/__   SUN   MON   TUE   WED   THU   FRI   SAT

Anxiety
Notes

ACTIVITY LEVEL

MOOD

ENERGY

SLEEP

SYMPTOMS

TRIGGERS

COPING SKILLS

MINDFULNESS EXERCISES

DATE: __/__/__   SUN   MON   TUE   WED   THU   FRI   SAT

Anxiety
Notes

ACTIVITY LEVEL

MOOD

ENERGY

SLEEP

TRIGGERS

SYMPTOMS

COPING SKILLS

MINDFULNESS EXERCISES

DATE: __/__/__   SUN   MON   TUE   WED   THU   FRI   SAT

Anxiety Notes

ACTIVITY LEVEL

MOOD

ENERGY

SLEEP

SYMPTOMS

TRIGGERS

COPING SKILLS

MINDFULNESS EXERCISES

DATE: __/__/__   SUN   MON   TUE   WED   THU   FRI   SAT

Anxiety Notes

ACTIVITY LEVEL

MOOD

ENERGY

SLEEP

TRIGGERS

SYMPTOMS

COPING SKILLS

MINDFULNESS EXERCISES

DATE: __/__/__   SUN   MON   TUE   WED   THU   FRI   SAT

Anxiety
Notes

ACTIVITY LEVEL

MOOD

ENERGY

SLEEP

SYMPTOMS

TRIGGERS

COPING SKILLS

MINDFULNESS EXERCISES

DATE: __/__/__   SUN   MON   TUE   WED   THU   FRI   SAT

Anxiety
Notes

ACTIVITY LEVEL

MOOD

ENERGY

SLEEP

TRIGGERS

SYMPTOMS

COPING SKILLS

MINDFULNESS EXERCISES

DATE: __/__/__   SUN   MON   TUE   WED   THU   FRI   SAT

Anxiety
Notes

ACTIVITY LEVEL

MOOD

ENERGY

SLEEP

SYMPTOMS

TRIGGERS

COPING SKILLS

MINDFULNESS EXERCISES

DATE: __/__/__   SUN   MON   TUE   WED   THU   FRI   SAT

Anxiety
Notes

ACTIVITY LEVEL

MOOD

ENERGY

SLEEP

TRIGGERS

SYMPTOMS

COPING SKILLS

MINDFULNESS EXERCISES

DATE: __/__/__   SUN   MON   TUE   WED   THU   FRI   SAT

Anxiety
Notes

ACTIVITY LEVEL

MOOD

ENERGY

SLEEP

SYMPTOMS

TRIGGERS

COPING SKILLS

MINDFULNESS EXERCISES

DATE: __/__/__   SUN   MON   TUE   WED   THU   FRI   SAT

Anxiety
Notes

ACTIVITY LEVEL

MOOD

ENERGY

SLEEP

TRIGGERS

SYMPTOMS

COPING SKILLS

MINDFULNESS EXERCISES

DATE: __/__/__   SUN   MON   TUE   WED   THU   FRI   SAT

Anxiety
Notes

ACTIVITY LEVEL

MOOD

ENERGY

SLEEP

SYMPTOMS

TRIGGERS

COPING SKILLS

MINDFULNESS EXERCISES

DATE: __/__/__   SUN   MON   TUE   WED   THU   FRI   SAT

Anxiety
Notes

ACTIVITY LEVEL

MOOD

ENERGY

SLEEP

TRIGGERS

SYMPTOMS

COPING SKILLS

MINDFULNESS EXERCISES

DATE: __/__/__   SUN   MON   TUE   WED   THU   FRI   SAT

Anxiety Notes

— ACTIVITY LEVEL —

— MOOD —

— ENERGY —

— SLEEP —

— SYMPTOMS —

— TRIGGERS —

— COPING SKILLS —

— MINDFULNESS EXERCISES —

DATE: __/__/__   SUN   MON   TUE   WED   THU   FRI   SAT

Anxiety
Notes

ACTIVITY LEVEL

MOOD

ENERGY

SLEEP

TRIGGERS

SYMPTOMS

COPING SKILLS

MINDFULNESS EXERCISES

DATE: __/__/__   SUN   MON   TUE   WED   THU   FRI   SAT

Anxiety
Notes

ACTIVITY LEVEL

MOOD

ENERGY

SLEEP

SYMPTOMS

TRIGGERS

COPING SKILLS

MINDFULNESS EXERCISES

DATE: __/__/__   SUN   MON   TUE   WED   THU   FRI   SAT

Anxiety Notes

ACTIVITY LEVEL

MOOD

ENERGY

SLEEP

TRIGGERS

SYMPTOMS

COPING SKILLS

MINDFULNESS EXERCISES

DATE: __/__/__   SUN   MON   TUE   WED   THU   FRI   SAT

Anxiety
Notes

ACTIVITY LEVEL

MOOD

ENERGY

SLEEP

SYMPTOMS

TRIGGERS

COPING SKILLS

MINDFULNESS EXERCISES

DATE: __/__/__   SUN   MON   TUE   WED   THU   FRI   SAT

Anxiety
Notes

ACTIVITY LEVEL

MOOD

ENERGY

SLEEP

TRIGGERS

SYMPTOMS

COPING SKILLS

MINDFULNESS EXERCISES

DATE: __/__/__   SUN   MON   TUE   WED   THU   FRI   SAT

Anxiety
Notes

ACTIVITY LEVEL

MOOD

ENERGY

SLEEP

SYMPTOMS

TRIGGERS

COPING SKILLS

MINDFULNESS EXERCISES

DATE: __/__/__   SUN   MON   TUE   WED   THU   FRI   SAT

Anxiety
Notes

ACTIVITY LEVEL

MOOD

ENERGY

SLEEP

TRIGGERS

SYMPTOMS

COPING SKILLS

MINDFULNESS EXERCISES

DATE: __/__/__   SUN   MON   TUE   WED   THU   FRI   SAT

Anxiety
Notes

ACTIVITY LEVEL

MOOD

ENERGY

SLEEP

SYMPTOMS

TRIGGERS

COPING SKILLS

MINDFULNESS EXERCISES

DATE: __/__/__   SUN   MON   TUE   WED   THU   FRI   SAT

Anxiety
Notes

ACTIVITY LEVEL

MOOD

ENERGY

SLEEP

TRIGGERS

SYMPTOMS

COPING SKILLS

MINDFULNESS EXERCISES

DATE: __/__/__   SUN   MON   TUE   WED   THU   FRI   SAT

Anxiety Notes

ACTIVITY LEVEL

MOOD

ENERGY

SLEEP

SYMPTOMS

_____
_____
_____
_____
_____
_____
_____

TRIGGERS

_____
_____
_____

COPING SKILLS

_____
_____
_____

MINDFULNESS EXERCISES

_____
_____
_____
_____
_____
_____
_____
_____

DATE: __/__/__   SUN   MON   TUE   WED   THU   FRI   SAT

Anxiety
Notes

ACTIVITY LEVEL

MOOD

ENERGY

SLEEP

TRIGGERS

SYMPTOMS

COPING SKILLS

MINDFULNESS EXERCISES

DATE: __/__/__   SUN   MON   TUE   WED   THU   FRI   SAT

Anxiety Notes

ACTIVITY LEVEL

MOOD

ENERGY

SLEEP

SYMPTOMS

TRIGGERS

COPING SKILLS

MINDFULNESS EXERCISES

DATE: __/__/__   SUN   MON   TUE   WED   THU   FRI   SAT

Anxiety
Notes

ACTIVITY LEVEL

MOOD   ENERGY   SLEEP

TRIGGERS   SYMPTOMS

COPING SKILLS

MINDFULNESS EXERCISES

DATE: __/__/__   SUN   MON   TUE   WED   THU   FRI   SAT

Anxiety
Notes

┌─── ACTIVITY LEVEL ───┐

┌─── MOOD ───┐ ┌─── ENERGY ───┐ ┌─── SLEEP ───┐

┌─── SYMPTOMS ───┐ ┌─── TRIGGERS ───┐

┌─── COPING SKILLS ───┐

┌─── MINDFULNESS EXERCISES ───┐

DATE: __/__/__   SUN   MON   TUE   WED   THU   FRI   SAT

Anxiety
Notes

ACTIVITY LEVEL

MOOD

ENERGY

SLEEP

TRIGGERS

SYMPTOMS

COPING SKILLS

MINDFULNESS EXERCISES

DATE: __/__/__   SUN   MON   TUE   WED   THU   FRI   SAT

Anxiety
Notes

ACTIVITY LEVEL

MOOD

ENERGY

SLEEP

SYMPTOMS

TRIGGERS

COPING SKILLS

MINDFULNESS EXERCISES

DATE: __/__/__   SUN   MON   TUE   WED   THU   FRI   SAT

Anxiety
Notes

ACTIVITY LEVEL

MOOD

ENERGY

SLEEP

TRIGGERS

SYMPTOMS

COPING SKILLS

MINDFULNESS EXERCISES

DATE: __/__/__   SUN   MON   TUE   WED   THU   FRI   SAT

Anxiety
Notes

ACTIVITY LEVEL

MOOD

ENERGY

SLEEP

SYMPTOMS

TRIGGERS

COPING SKILLS

MINDFULNESS EXERCISES

DATE: __/__/__   SUN   MON   TUE   WED   THU   FRI   SAT

Anxiety
Notes

ACTIVITY LEVEL

MOOD

ENERGY

SLEEP

TRIGGERS

SYMPTOMS

COPING SKILLS

MINDFULNESS EXERCISES

DATE: __/__/__   SUN   MON   TUE   WED   THU   FRI   SAT

Anxiety
Notes

ACTIVITY LEVEL

MOOD

ENERGY

SLEEP

SYMPTOMS

TRIGGERS

COPING SKILLS

MINDFULNESS EXERCISES

DATE: __/__/__   SUN   MON   TUE   WED   THU   FRI   SAT

Anxiety
Notes

ACTIVITY LEVEL

MOOD

ENERGY

SLEEP

TRIGGERS

SYMPTOMS

COPING SKILLS

MINDFULNESS EXERCISES

DATE: __/__/__   SUN   MON   TUE   WED   THU   FRI   SAT

Anxiety Notes

ACTIVITY LEVEL

MOOD

ENERGY

SLEEP

SYMPTOMS

TRIGGERS

COPING SKILLS

MINDFULNESS EXERCISES

DATE: __/__/__   SUN   MON   TUE   WED   THU   FRI   SAT

Anxiety
Notes

┌─── ACTIVITY LEVEL ───┐

┌─── MOOD ───┐   ┌─── ENERGY ───┐   ┌─── SLEEP ───┐

┌─── TRIGGERS ───┐   ┌─── SYMPTOMS ───┐

┌─── COPING SKILLS ───┐

┌─── MINDFULNESS EXERCISES ───┐

DATE: __/__/__   SUN   MON   TUE   WED   THU   FRI   SAT

Anxiety Notes

ACTIVITY LEVEL

MOOD

ENERGY

SLEEP

SYMPTOMS

TRIGGERS

COPING SKILLS

MINDFULNESS EXERCISES

DATE: __/__/__   SUN   MON   TUE   WED   THU   FRI   SAT

Anxiety
Notes

ACTIVITY LEVEL

MOOD

ENERGY

SLEEP

TRIGGERS

SYMPTOMS

COPING SKILLS

MINDFULNESS EXERCISES

DATE: __/__/__   SUN   MON   TUE   WED   THU   FRI   SAT

Anxiety Notes

ACTIVITY LEVEL

MOOD

ENERGY

SLEEP

SYMPTOMS

TRIGGERS

COPING SKILLS

MINDFULNESS EXERCISES

DATE: __/__/__   SUN   MON   TUE   WED   THU   FRI   SAT

Anxiety
Notes

ACTIVITY LEVEL

MOOD

ENERGY

SLEEP

TRIGGERS

SYMPTOMS

COPING SKILLS

MINDFULNESS EXERCISES

DATE: __/__/__   SUN   MON   TUE   WED   THU   FRI   SAT

Anxiety
Notes

ACTIVITY LEVEL

MOOD

ENERGY

SLEEP

SYMPTOMS

TRIGGERS

COPING SKILLS

MINDFULNESS EXERCISES

DATE: __/__/__   SUN   MON   TUE   WED   THU   FRI   SAT

Anxiety Notes

ACTIVITY LEVEL

MOOD

ENERGY

SLEEP

TRIGGERS

SYMPTOMS

COPING SKILLS

MINDFULNESS EXERCISES

DATE: __/__/__   SUN   MON   TUE   WED   THU   FRI   SAT

Anxiety
Notes

ACTIVITY LEVEL

MOOD

ENERGY

SLEEP

SYMPTOMS

TRIGGERS

COPING SKILLS

MINDFULNESS EXERCISES

DATE: __/__/__   SUN   MON   TUE   WED   THU   FRI   SAT

Anxiety
Notes

ACTIVITY LEVEL

MOOD

ENERGY

SLEEP

TRIGGERS

SYMPTOMS

COPING SKILLS

MINDFULNESS EXERCISES

DATE: __/__/__   SUN   MON   TUE   WED   THU   FRI   SAT

Anxiety
Notes

ACTIVITY LEVEL

MOOD

ENERGY

SLEEP

SYMPTOMS

TRIGGERS

COPING SKILLS

MINDFULNESS EXERCISES

DATE: __/__/__ SUN   MON   TUE   WED   THU   FRI   SAT

Anxiety
Notes

ACTIVITY LEVEL

MOOD

ENERGY

SLEEP

TRIGGERS

SYMPTOMS

COPING SKILLS

MINDFULNESS EXERCISES

DATE: __/__/__   SUN   MON   TUE   WED   THU   FRI   SAT

Anxiety
Notes

ACTIVITY LEVEL

MOOD

ENERGY

SLEEP

SYMPTOMS

TRIGGERS

COPING SKILLS

MINDFULNESS EXERCISES

DATE: __/__/__   SUN   MON   TUE   WED   THU   FRI   SAT

Anxiety
Notes

ACTIVITY LEVEL

MOOD

ENERGY

SLEEP

TRIGGERS

SYMPTOMS

COPING SKILLS

MINDFULNESS EXERCISES

DATE: __/__/__   SUN   MON   TUE   WED   THU   FRI   SAT

Anxiety
Notes

ACTIVITY LEVEL

MOOD

ENERGY

SLEEP

SYMPTOMS

TRIGGERS

COPING SKILLS

MINDFULNESS EXERCISES

DATE: __/__/__   SUN   MON   TUE   WED   THU   FRI   SAT

Anxiety
Notes

ACTIVITY LEVEL

MOOD

ENERGY

SLEEP

TRIGGERS

_____
_____
_____

SYMPTOMS

_____
_____
_____
_____
_____
_____
_____

COPING SKILLS

_____
_____
_____

MINDFULNESS EXERCISES

_____
_____
_____
_____
_____
_____
_____
_____

DATE: __/__/__   SUN   MON   TUE   WED   THU   FRI   SAT

Anxiety
Notes

ACTIVITY LEVEL

MOOD

ENERGY

SLEEP

SYMPTOMS

TRIGGERS

COPING SKILLS

MINDFULNESS EXERCISES

DATE: __/__/__   SUN   MON   TUE   WED   THU   FRI   SAT

Anxiety Notes

ACTIVITY LEVEL

MOOD

ENERGY

SLEEP

TRIGGERS

SYMPTOMS

COPING SKILLS

MINDFULNESS EXERCISES

DATE: __/__/__   SUN   MON   TUE   WED   THU   FRI   SAT

Anxiety Notes

ACTIVITY LEVEL

MOOD

ENERGY

SLEEP

SYMPTOMS

TRIGGERS

COPING SKILLS

MINDFULNESS EXERCISES

DATE: __/__/__   SUN   MON   TUE   WED   THU   FRI   SAT

Anxiety
Notes

ACTIVITY LEVEL

MOOD

ENERGY

SLEEP

TRIGGERS

SYMPTOMS

COPING SKILLS

MINDFULNESS EXERCISES

DATE: __/__/__   SUN   MON   TUE   WED   THU   FRI   SAT

Anxiety
Notes

ACTIVITY LEVEL

MOOD

ENERGY

SLEEP

SYMPTOMS

TRIGGERS

COPING SKILLS

MINDFULNESS EXERCISES

DATE: __/__/__   SUN   MON   TUE   WED   THU   FRI   SAT

Anxiety Notes

ACTIVITY LEVEL

MOOD

ENERGY

SLEEP

TRIGGERS

SYMPTOMS

COPING SKILLS

MINDFULNESS EXERCISES

DATE: __/__/__   SUN   MON   TUE   WED   THU   FRI   SAT

Anxiety
Notes

ACTIVITY LEVEL

MOOD

ENERGY

SLEEP

SYMPTOMS

TRIGGERS

COPING SKILLS

MINDFULNESS EXERCISES

DATE: __/__/__   SUN   MON   TUE   WED   THU   FRI   SAT

Anxiety Notes

ACTIVITY LEVEL

MOOD

ENERGY

SLEEP

TRIGGERS

SYMPTOMS

COPING SKILLS

MINDFULNESS EXERCISES

DATE: __/__/__   SUN   MON   TUE   WED   THU   FRI   SAT

Anxiety Notes

ACTIVITY LEVEL

MOOD

ENERGY

SLEEP

SYMPTOMS

TRIGGERS

COPING SKILLS

MINDFULNESS EXERCISES

DATE: __/__/__   SUN   MON   TUE   WED   THU   FRI   SAT

Anxiety
Notes

ACTIVITY LEVEL

MOOD

ENERGY

SLEEP

TRIGGERS

SYMPTOMS

COPING SKILLS

MINDFULNESS EXERCISES

DATE: __/__/__   SUN   MON   TUE   WED   THU   FRI   SAT

Anxiety
Notes

ACTIVITY LEVEL

MOOD

ENERGY

SLEEP

SYMPTOMS

TRIGGERS

COPING SKILLS

MINDFULNESS EXERCISES

DATE: __/__/__   SUN   MON   TUE   WED   THU   FRI   SAT

Anxiety
Notes

ACTIVITY LEVEL

MOOD

ENERGY

SLEEP

TRIGGERS

SYMPTOMS

COPING SKILLS

MINDFULNESS EXERCISES

DATE: __/__/__   SUN   MON   TUE   WED   THU   FRI   SAT

Anxiety
Notes

ACTIVITY LEVEL

MOOD

ENERGY

SLEEP

SYMPTOMS

_____
_____
_____
_____
_____
_____
_____

TRIGGERS

_____
_____
_____

COPING SKILLS

_____
_____
_____

MINDFULNESS EXERCISES

_____
_____
_____
_____
_____
_____
_____
_____

DATE: __/__/__   SUN   MON   TUE   WED   THU   FRI   SAT

Anxiety
Notes

ACTIVITY LEVEL

MOOD

ENERGY

SLEEP

TRIGGERS

SYMPTOMS

COPING SKILLS

MINDFULNESS EXERCISES

DATE: __/__/__   SUN   MON   TUE   WED   THU   FRI   SAT

Anxiety
Notes

ACTIVITY LEVEL

MOOD

ENERGY

SLEEP

SYMPTOMS

TRIGGERS

COPING SKILLS

MINDFULNESS EXERCISES

DATE: __/__/__   SUN   MON   TUE   WED   THU   FRI   SAT

Anxiety Notes

ACTIVITY LEVEL

MOOD

ENERGY

SLEEP

TRIGGERS

SYMPTOMS

COPING SKILLS

MINDFULNESS EXERCISES

DATE: __/__/__   SUN   MON   TUE   WED   THU   FRI   SAT

Anxiety
Notes

ACTIVITY LEVEL

MOOD

ENERGY

SLEEP

SYMPTOMS

TRIGGERS

COPING SKILLS

MINDFULNESS EXERCISES

DATE: __/__/__   SUN   MON   TUE   WED   THU   FRI   SAT

Anxiety
Notes

ACTIVITY LEVEL

MOOD

ENERGY

SLEEP

TRIGGERS

SYMPTOMS

COPING SKILLS

MINDFULNESS EXERCISES

DATE: __/__/__   SUN   MON   TUE   WED   THU   FRI   SAT

Anxiety Notes

ACTIVITY LEVEL

MOOD

ENERGY

SLEEP

SYMPTOMS

_____
_____
_____
_____
_____
_____
_____

TRIGGERS

_____
_____
_____

COPING SKILLS

_____
_____
_____

MINDFULNESS EXERCISES

_____
_____
_____
_____
_____
_____
_____
_____

DATE: __/__/__   SUN   MON   TUE   WED   THU   FRI   SAT

Anxiety Notes

ACTIVITY LEVEL

MOOD

ENERGY

SLEEP

TRIGGERS

SYMPTOMS

COPING SKILLS

MINDFULNESS EXERCISES

Made in the USA
Monee, IL
11 February 2023

27514811R00057